PRIVATE LESSONS

by Robert Clava

PLAYBACK+
Speed • Pitch • Balance • Loop

To access audio visit:
www.halleonard.com/mylibrary

Enter Code
2200-1365-0513-7787

ISBN 978-0-7935-9964-6

7777 W. BLUEMOUND RD. P.O. BOX 13819 MILWAUKEE, WI 53213

Visit Hal Leonard Online at
www.halleonard.com

DEDICATION

This book is dedicated to my parents for their love, understanding, compassion, and support throughout the years. To Lt. Col. R.B. Theime, Jr. for his faithful teaching of the Word of God, which has had (and continues to have) a profound influence on my life. And to Johnny Winter, who inspired me to play the blues in the first place.

ACKNOWLEDGMENTS

A very special thanks to David Oakes, Paul Hanson, Owen Goldman, and Bruce Buckingham, who helped out in various aspects of making this book and audio pack. I could not have done it without your help!

TABLE OF CONTENTS

PREFACE

Before you begin your study of this book/audio pack, you should at least be familiar with open position chords, barre chords, and basic string-bending techniques. Although this book is designed for the beginning to intermediate player, you will get much more out of it if you have those basic skills. If you are unfamiliar with the material mentioned above, you can still benefit from this book, although some of the solos and rhythm parts may be harder for you to play at first (for a good book on basic guitar technique, check out *Guitar Basics* by Bruce Buckingham). Also, if you can read music on the guitar, this will help you learn the music much more quickly. You can still get a lot out of this book by using your ear and reading the tablature staff. But, once again, you will get more out of the material and will be able to learn it faster if you can read a bit already (a very good book on reading is *Music Reading for Guitar* by David Oakes). So, if you have played for a while and can read a little, dig in and enjoy! If not, go slowly, and do the best you can. Either way, your efforts will be rewarded, and you will get a lot out of this book/audio pack. Keep on pickin' and a grinnin'!

Robert Calva

HOW TO USE THIS BOOK

This book is the result of my having worked with various and sundry students over the years, helping them learn how to play the blues. This book is not exhaustive by any means but is a primer to the Texas blues guitar style. You will notice that there is some material in this book from players who are not from Texas. This is because Texas blues itself contains elements of Delta blues and Chicago blues as well as elements that are unique to players from Texas. For me to give an example of a lick or phrase and say it was from Stevie Ray Vaughan when, in reality, Stevie learned it from Albert King would be a great disservice to Albert King. It also ignores the fact that, ever since recorded music became readily available in the U.S. and around the world, aspiring blues musicians everywhere have been learning things primarily from recordings resulting in the fact that many Texas blues players were, and still are, influenced by many non-Texas players. The history of blues is full of artists borrowing or "stealing" musical ideas from each other!

I have tried to put the material in this book into a form that is easy to understand, easy to learn, and that makes sense. Although there is no substitute to working with a good teacher, I have tried to design this book/audio pack so that working with it can be done without the aid of an instructor. You should learn both the solos and the rhythm parts as close to the recording as you can. You can use the play-along tracks to work on both your rhythm playing and your soloing. The rhythm tracks have been hard-panned to the right and left channels so you can listen closely to each part and play along with it, or play along with one part while you listen to the other. You will notice several embellishments to the rhythm parts on the audio tracks. Some of these have been included in the rhythm parts as *rhythm fills*. Others are simply subtle variations on the written parts, used to add variety. Listen closely for these and try to adopt them into your own rhythm playing once you have learned the written parts. I cannot stress enough the importance of being a good, solid rhythm player. The better rhythm player you are, the better soloist you will be. Your soloing will have better rhythm, and you'll develop a better sense of phrasing. So, learn and memorize the rhythm parts to each solo first before you start learning and memorizing the solos.

I have designed the solos to help teach blues phrasing, how to state a melodic idea and develop it, and solo structure in general. (I will discuss these elements in greater detail in the "Parting Words" section of this book.) You can use the rhythm tracks to practice the written solos and to work on your own solos using the licks, phrases, and ideas that you like from the written solos.

And now, without any further ado, let's get into the music! I hope you have as much fun learning this material as I did in putting it together.

Common Blues "Box" Positions

Most beginning blues players try to approach improvising over a blues progression by learning the blues scale all over the neck. Although there is nothing wrong with this approach, it usually does not yield the best results. Rather than trying to learn all five patterns of the blues scale all over the neck (which can be very tedious), the beginning blues player will get better results (bluesier sounds) by first learning some of the more common blues "box" positions used by many of the great blues guitarists. After this has been done, it is then easy to relate the box positions with the five patterns of the blues scale all over the finger-board to get a more complete picture of the fretboard (for a more in-depth discussion on the five different scale patterns, see *Guitar Soloing* by Dan Gilbert and Beth Marlis).

So as not to confuse them with the other scale patterns, we will use the letter "B" (for "box") in addition to the scale pattern numbers to identify the different box positions. Please remember that all these box positions are shown here in the key of A.

Box 4B is probably the most familiar to you. Start with your third finger on the fourth string, seventh fret; your first finger should be on the fifth fret (fifth position), and keep one finger per fret. This box position is the second octave of a pattern 4 blues scale.

Fig. 1 – Box 4B

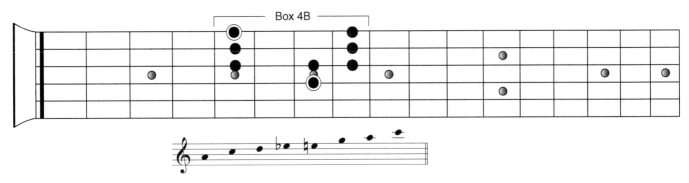

Box 5B provides us with many traditional blues licks and sounds and is used almost exclusively by a host of great players. Start with your second finger on the third string, ninth fret; your first finger should be on the eighth fret (eighth position). This box position comes from the upper octave of a pattern 5 blues scale.

Fig. 2 – Box 5B

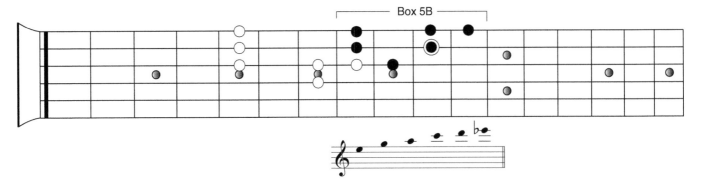

Box 1B begins with a similar fingering to box 5B. To play this box pattern correctly, slide with your third finger from B on the second string at the twelfth fret up to the C♯ on the second string at the fourteenth fret. This puts your first finger on the twelfth fret. You can also bend up to the notes that are out of position. This box position is a combination of the upper octaves of major pentatonic scale patterns 1 and 2.

Fig. 3 – Box 1B

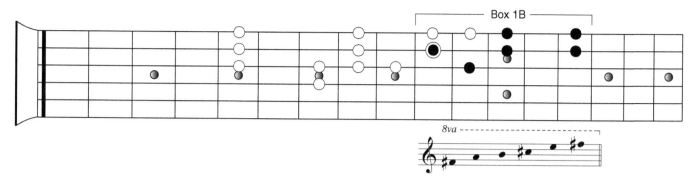

Box 2B shares nearly the same fingering as box 1B (E♭ is added) and is played in a similar manner. This box position comes from the second octave of a pattern 2 blues scale with two notes from a pattern 4 blues scale. Please note that this box position is found in two places on the fingerboard in the key of A (first position and thirteenth position).

Fig. 4 – Box 2B

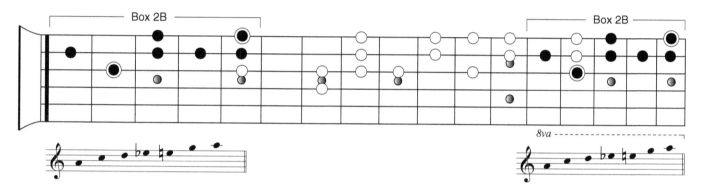

Box 3B uses a similar fingering to box 4B and has a more "uptown" major sound to it. That is because it comes from the second octave of a pattern 3 major pentatonic scale. This box position is also found in two areas of the fingerboard in the key of A (second and fourteenth position).

Fig. 5 – Box 3B

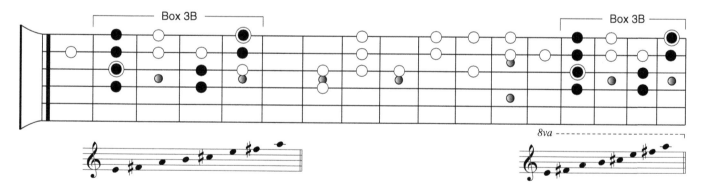

Each box position should be learned individually. After you have learned them separately, it is easy to connect them since most of the positions share the same fingerings. The roots are circled, and the white dots show you how each box position relates to the previous one. Once these boxes have been learned in the key of A, it is easy to transpose to different keys; you just have to move the boxes up or down the fretboard for the desired key. Transposing will be discussed briefly at the conclusion of this book. After you have these box shapes underneath your fingers, feel free to try them out over the play-along rhythm tracks. Experiment and have fun!

2 Twenty-Four Common Blues Licks

Now that you have learned the box positions, we'll look at some licks that are found in each position.

Licks 1-10 are basic blues-rock licks that most players should know. Licks 11-24 are a little more advanced licks that combine a few of the first ten licks into short phrases. All of these licks (and more!) are used in the solos in this book, so learn them well before you start to learn the solos.

Lick 1 is a whole-step bend from D up to E in box 4B with your third finger. Be sure to use your first and second fingers to help support your third finger in the bend. For variety, try bending up a half step to E♭ instead of E; this will give you the ♭5 (one of the "blue" notes).

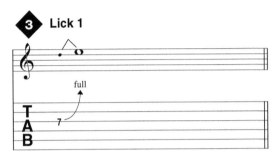

The notes in lick 2 can be played either separately or together. Make sure that the bent note matches the pitch of the fretted note.

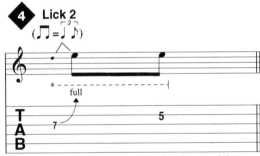

*These notes are played together the second time.

The notes in lick 3 can also be played both separately and together as well. This a favorite of many great blues players including the late and truly great Stevie Ray Vaughan (SRV).

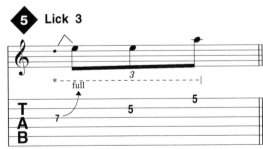

*These notes are played together the second time.

Lick 4 can also be played both with the notes separately and together. Players such as Freddie King, Johnny Winter, SRV, and countless others have done some very cool things with this lick.

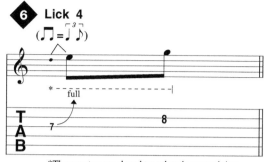

*These notes are played together the second time.

Lick 5 is a whole-step bend from the ♭7 (G), another "blue" note, to the root (A).

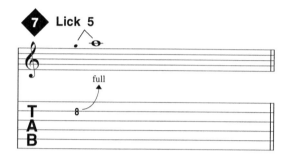

Once again, the notes in lick 6 can be played both separately and together. SRV, Johnny Winter, and many others have done great things with this!

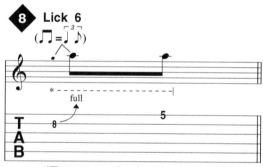

*These notes are played together the second time.

Lick 7 is a major-sounding lick that has a bit of a country flavor to it. Keep the note on the first string fretted with your fourth finger without bending it. Again, you can play the notes separately or together.

*These notes are played together the second time.

Lick 8 is a whole-step bend from C (the ♭3rd, another "blue" note) up to D on the first string with your third finger.

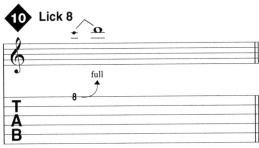

Lick 9 requires you to make a half barre with your first and third fingers.

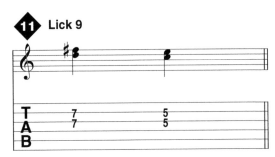

Lick 10 is a variation of lick 9. Pre-bend the second and third strings down towards the floor with your third finger, pick the strings, and then release the bend quickly to play the D and F♯ notes.

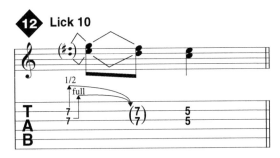

Lick 11 is a very common lick used by almost every blues player and combines licks 3 and 5. It is also a great lick to start a solo with.

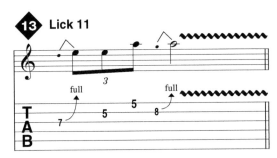

Lick 12 is a variation of lick 11.

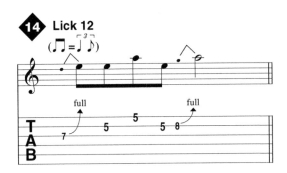

Lick 13 is an Albert King lick that was also used a lot by the late Stevie Ray Vaughan. Notice how a slide is used from G up to A instead of a bend.

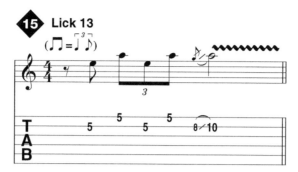

Lick 14 is an Albert King lick by way of SRV; check out "The Sky Is Cryin'" by SRV. Make sure you make the bend from D to E very short and staccato.

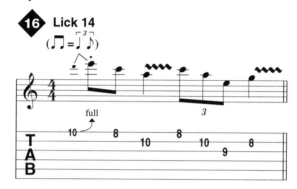

Lick 15 is another classic Albert King/SRV lick. Be careful not to overbend the quarter-step bend on the last two notes of the first measure.

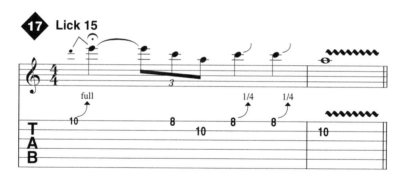

Lick 16 is a classic B.B. King lick. Yes, I know that B.B. King is not from Texas, but he's influenced so many great Texas players that I had to include a lick or two from him. Make sure you nail the half-step bend.

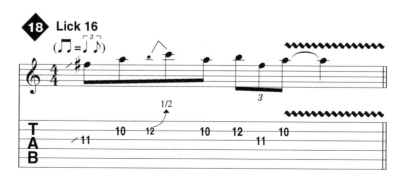

Lick 17 is everybody's favorite! It's another Albert King lick that's been used by SRV and others. Make sure you get the minor and major 3rd bends on beats 1 and 4. Actually, the first bend (E-G) sounds better if you bend up to the note between F♯ and G, which means you want to bend a little bit higher than F♯ but not quite up to G. It sounds more authentic that way. Microtonal bends occur a lot in blues and are the result of guitarists trying to imitate blues singers who slur and slide into notes that are between the frets.

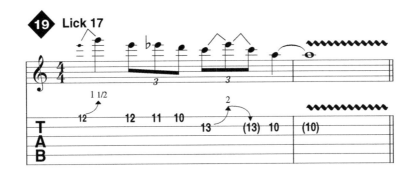

Lick 18 is from Muddy Waters and is also a favorite of Johnny Winter, SRV, and countless others.

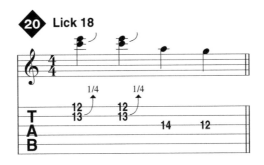

Lick 19 is another favorite of Johnny Winter and a host of other great players.

Lick 20 can also be played an octave higher in the fourteenth position and can be heard in Freddie King's "Hideaway."

Lick 21 combines both the major 3rd and the minor 3rd (C# and C♮) in one lick. This kind of ambiguity between the major and minor 3rd is quite common in the blues. As with lick 20, this lick can also be played in the fourteenth position.

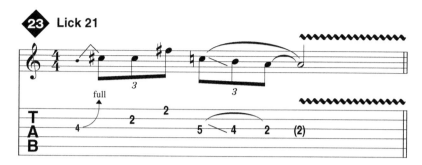

Lick 22 is in the style of Johnny Winter and SRV. Practice this one slowly with a metronome or drum machine before trying to play it fast.

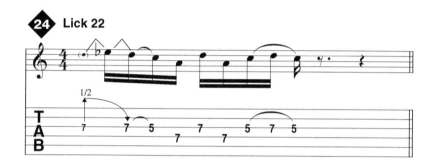

Lick 23 is another great lick I learned from Mr. Winter and have heard other players use as well. You can use your third or fourth finger to play the C note on the first string.

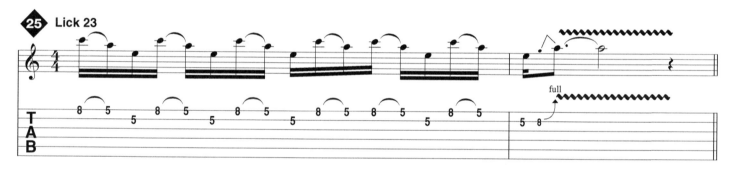

Lick 24 is another smokin' lick in the Johnny Winter/Stevie Ray vein. As with lick 22, play this one slowly and cleanly before trying to play it fast.

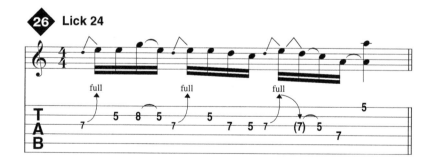

These licks should help you start developing your own blues vocabulary. Practice them slowly with a metronome, drum machine, or with the play-along rhythm tracks. Once you have these licks underneath your fingers, we will look at how to use them in the solos. Remember to do your research and listen to as many players as you can and keep on practicing and jamming.

3 The Blues Shuffle

The *blues shuffle* is the most common blues feel and groove. If you were to do a typical blues gig, chances are that most of the tunes you would play over the course of the night would be shuffles. Although there are different types of shuffles and numerous different ways to play them on the guitar, we are going to focus on one type of shuffle that is among the most common. The shuffle in this book is a medium-slow shuffle in the key of A. The rhythm tracks on the recording have two guitar parts that you should learn before you start learning the solos. Each rhythm part is hard-panned left and right so they are easy to listen and practice to. Learning the rhythm guitar parts will help you with your shuffle feel and phrasing.

Rhythm Guitar 1

This part is one that, if you do not already know it, you should become very familiar with. Remember to slightly mute the strings with the palm of your right hand (called palm muting, or "P.M.") throughout the entire part. Use all downstrokes, and do not be afraid to dig in hard and really hit the strings—you'll get a much better sound that way. Listen to Gtr. 1's part on the recording and play along with it. Do not worry so much about the embellishment figures on the fourth beat in measures 4 and 6-10. If you have trouble with them at first, just ignore them and concentrate on playing a good, solid groove. Once you get the basic part down, you can add the embellishment figures back in. The turnaround in measure 11 is a very common one that you should memorize and make part of your vocabulary of blues turnarounds. Once you get this part down, you can turn the balance knob on your stereo to the right and play along with Gtr. 2. Notice the walk-up to the IV chord (D7) that occurs in the fourth and eighth choruses of the blues shuffle rhythm track (Rhy. Fill 3). This walk-up is a very common device used to add variety and excitement to a blues progression, especially behind a soloist.

27 BLUES SHUFFLE RHYTHM 1

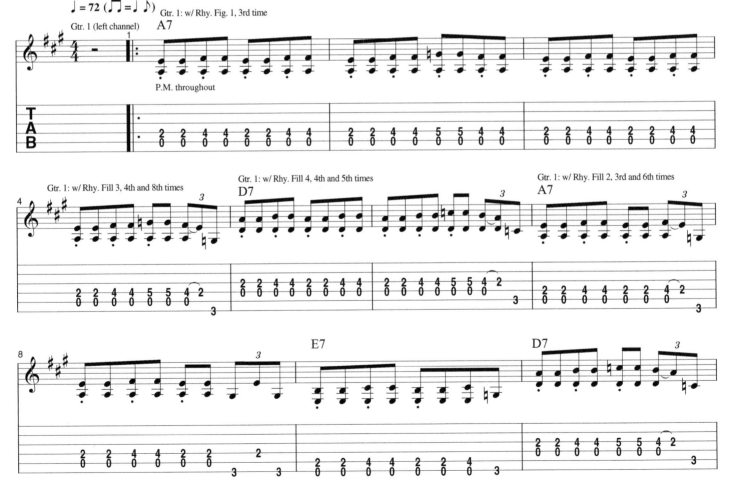

14

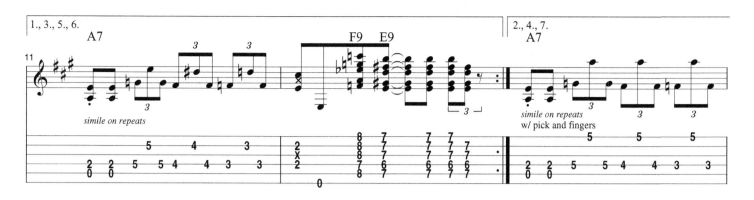

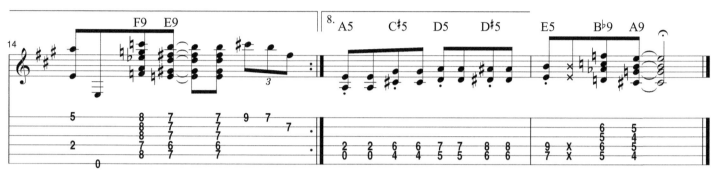

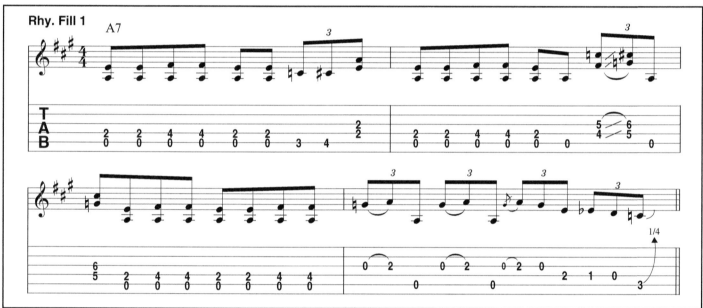

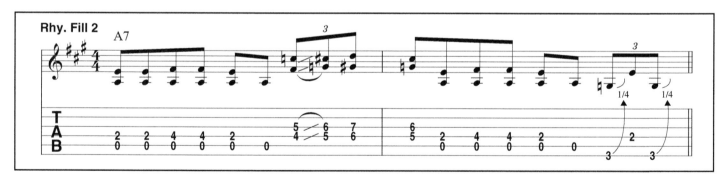

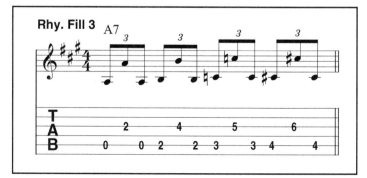

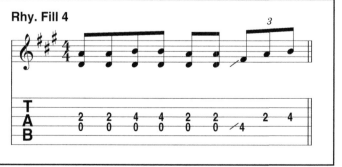

Rhythm Guitar 2

This part serves as a very nice complement to Gtr. 1. Guitar parts similar to these can be heard on the *Live at Carnegie Hall* album by Jimmy Reed. The right hand technique used to play this part is very similar to the one used to play SRV's "Pride and Joy," "Cold Shot," and all those other SRV Texas boogie shuffles. Move your right forearm in a circular motion very similar to the arm of a steam engine, "drawing" a circle around your neck pickup. Keep your right wrist loose and relaxed, and let most of the movement come from your elbow. It is very important to get the circular motion going. When your hand is in the downward swing of the circle, it strikes the muted strings on the downbeat. As your hand comes up toward the ceiling, the chord sounds on the upbeat. This is a lazy part and should be played a little behind the beat. If you are not loose and relaxed and do not play this part with a circular motion, then you will rush the part, sound stiff, and eventually get out of sync with the drums. Once you get this part down, you can turn the balance knob on your stereo to the left and play along with Gtr. 1. When you feel comfortable with both parts, you may start learning the solo.

27 BLUES SHUFFLE RHYTHM 2

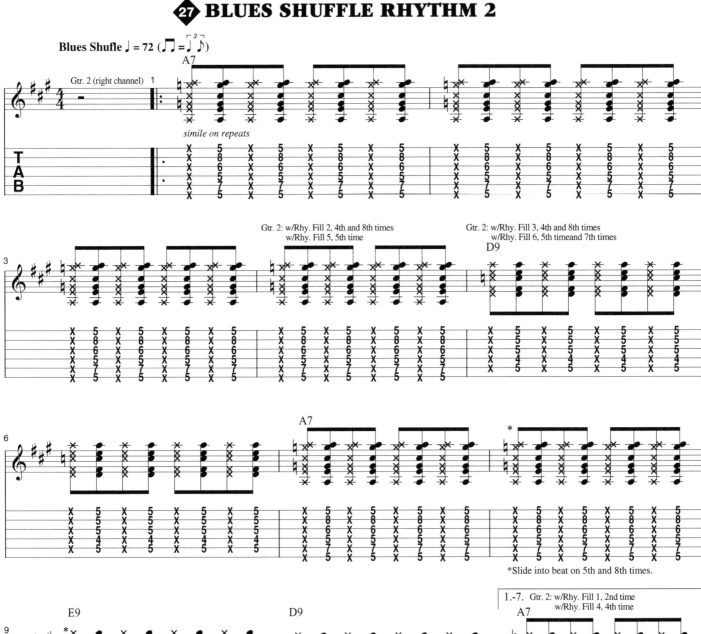

*Slide into first beat on 7th time.

16

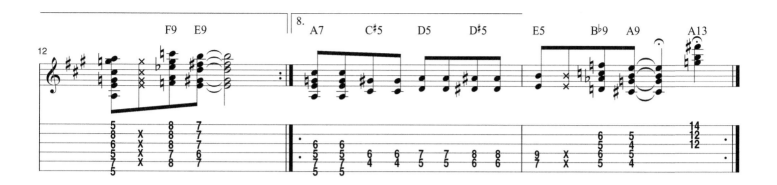

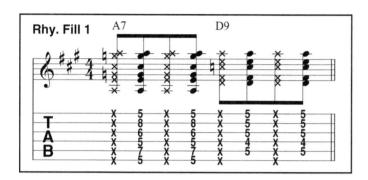

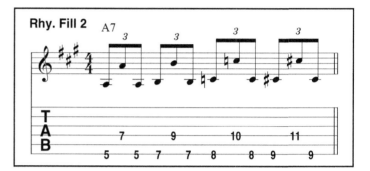

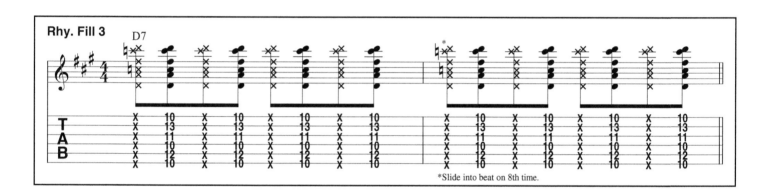

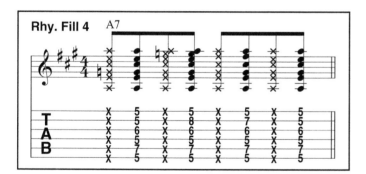

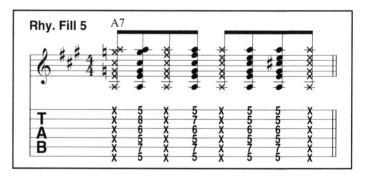

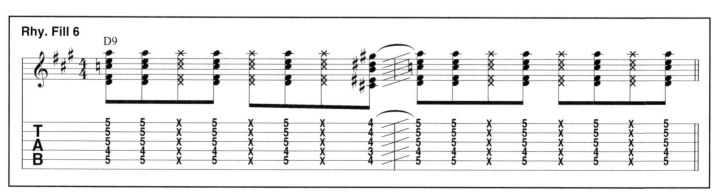

Blues Shuffle Solo

Now that you have learned the licks and have them underneath your fingers, it is time to put them to use! I have written a blues shuffle solo that should give you some ideas on how to use some of the twenty-four common blues licks. The solo is two choruses long, in the key of A, and is fairly easy to learn. Learn the solo as best as you can. Rely on your ear more than the written transcription to get some of the more subtle nuances. After you have learned and memorized the solo, you can use some of the ideas and phrases in your own solos. Try to be creative and come up with your own ideas over the rhythm track.

Chorus 1 opens up with a pickup figure that uses lick 1. The lick is repeated, becoming the opening melodic statement throughout the first three measures, and appears again in measure 9 on beat 3 and in measure 10 on beat 4 as part of a phrase. When playing lick 1 in measure 3, make sure your bends are accurate each time you bend up to E; the lick should sound the same each time. Lick 5 is used in measure 4 and is used throughout the rest of the chorus with some variations and added scale tones. In this chorus, pay particular attention to the phrasing and the use of space.

Chorus 2 opens with a figure that is a variation of the opening statement in chorus 1 and utilizes lick 4 throughout measures 13-15. In measure 16, there is a variation of lick 1 on beat 2—instead of bending up a whole step from D to E, D is only bent up a half step to E♭, the ♭5 of the I chord (A7). Measure 18 features a lick that has been used by countless blues players (Johnny Winter and SRV just to name a couple), which expands upon lick 5. Measures 19 and 20 use lick 9 with a slight variation. Measure 21 uses lick 5 with C (the ♭3 of A7) added on the first string, eighth fret on the "and" of beat 1. Lick 1 reappears starting on beat 3 of measure 21. Measure 22 features a line that comes from Jimmy Reed and Muddy Waters and was used often by Johnny Winter. Here it is played more in the style of Johnny Winter. Measures 23 and 24 contain a very typical blues ending lick that starts on beat 2 of measure 23. You should memorize this lick and make it part of your vocabulary of blues endings. Once again, as with chorus 1, pay particular attention to the phrasing and use of space.

◆28 BLUES SHUFFLE SOLO

Chorus 1
Medium Blues Shuffle ♩ = 72

*Use ending 1 of "Blues Shuffle Rhythm 1" for both parts.

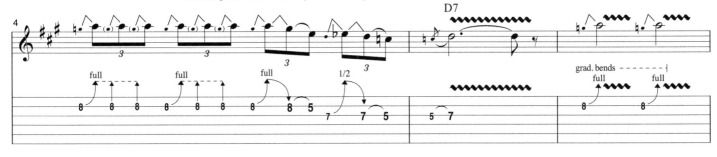

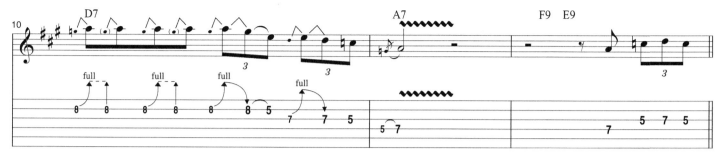

Chorus 2

*Gtr. 1: w/ Blues Shuffle Rhythm 1, simile
*Gtr. 2: w/ Blues Shuffle Rhythm 2, simile

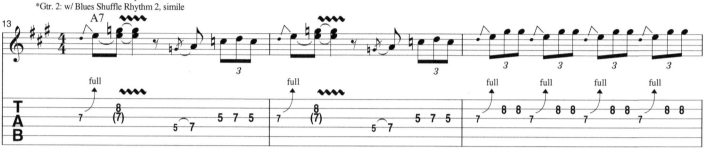

*Use ending 8.

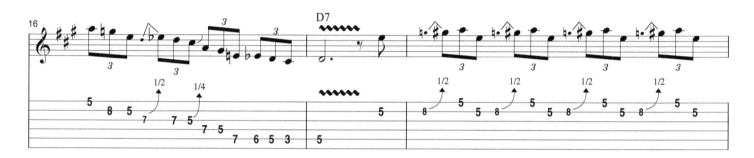

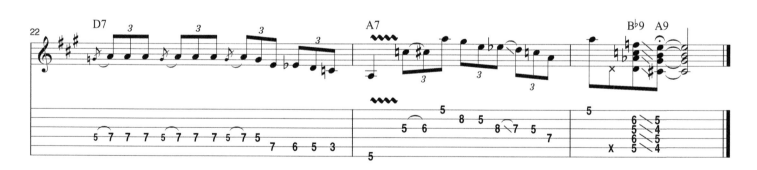

Slow Blues

The *slow blues* feel is another common blues groove that you will play over the course of an evening on a blues gig. Although most slow blues tunes have a 12/8 feel, I have written out the parts in 4/4 so they are easier to read. The slow blues example in this book is in the key of A. As with the shuffle tracks, the recording has two rhythm guitar parts that you should learn before you start learning the solos. Each rhythm part is panned hard left and right so they are easy to listen and practice to.

Rhythm Guitar 1

This part has some chord moves from various players. Most of the part is loosely based on the rhythm parts of T-Bone Walker from his recording of "Stormy Monday" and other slow blues tunes. The tricky thing about this part is the accent on the "and" of beat 4 in measures 2, 9, and 10. The chromatic walk-up to the IV chord in measure 4 on beat 3 occurs only in the first chorus. I learned this walk-up from Johnny Winter, and it can be heard in "You Keep Saying That You're Leaving" from his *Hey, Where's Your Brother* album and in the tune "Black Jack" from *Live in NYC '97*. This chromatic walk-up is a great way of adding variety to a slow blues progression. Also notice the chromatic descent from the IV chord back to the I chord in measure 6.

Another thing that makes this progression a little different is the use of the augmented V chord in measure 12, another nod to T-Bone Walker's "Stormy Monday." Since the chromatic walk-up does not occur in every chorus (it is not a device you want to overuse), for the rest of the choruses play the part for measures 4-6 that does not contain the walk-up (Rhy. Fill 1). The E♭9 with the added 13th embellishment on beat 4 of measure 4 is from T-Bone Walker. Listen to the Gtr. 1 part on the recording and play along with it. Once you get this part down, you can turn the balance knob on your stereo to the right and play along with Gtr. 2.

🔷29 SLOW BLUES RHYTHM 1

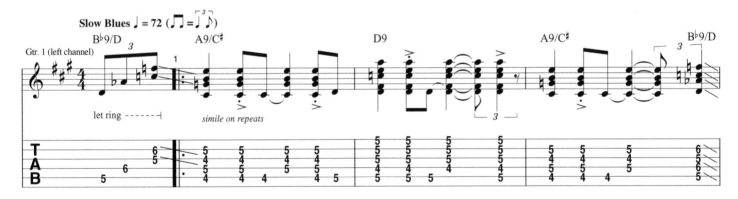

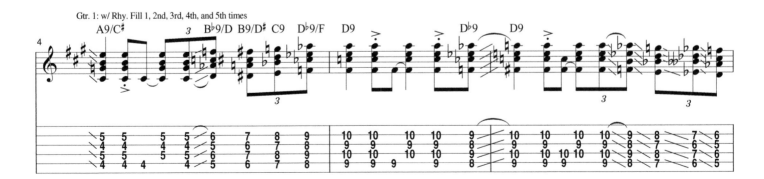

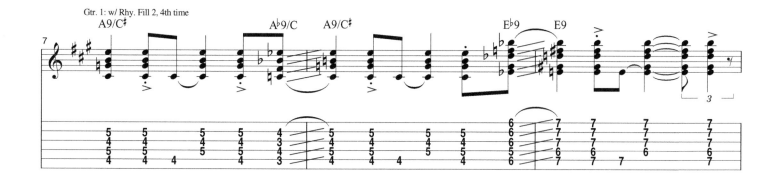

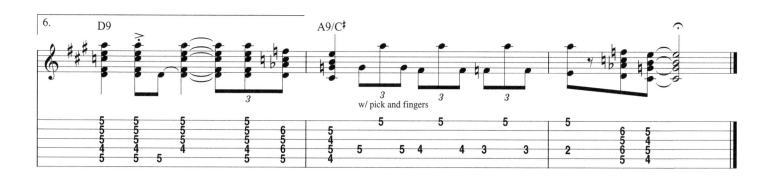

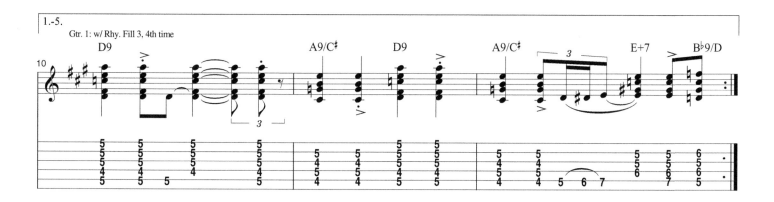

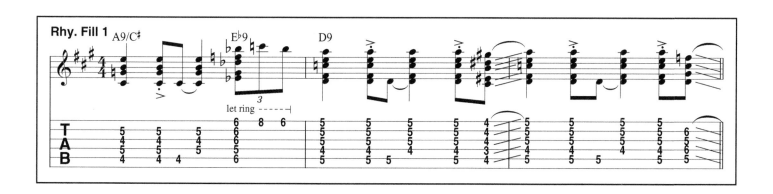

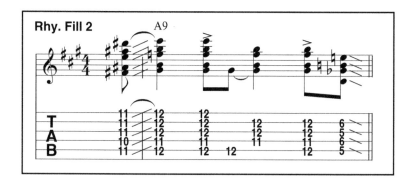

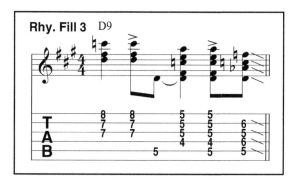

Rhythm Guitar 2

This part is based on something many piano players play with their right hand in a slow blues tune. When you play this part, strive to keep the triplets even and accent beats 2 and 4. There are a lot of good chord voicings and chord moves here that you should add to your vocabulary of blues comping ideas—in particular, the voicing of the V and IV chords in measures 9 and 10. As with Gtr. 1's part, the chromatic walk-up from the I to the IV chord only occurs in the first chorus. The passing chords on beat 4 of the first measure of Rhy. Fill 1 are a very nice way to take you from one chord voicing to another and are a common device used by many players. The 13th chord embellishment in the second measure of Rhy. Fill 1 is similar to the one in the Gtr. 1's part. For a different sound, try playing this with your right hand thumb instead of with a pick. Once you get this down, you can turn the balance knob on your stereo to the left and play along with Gtr. 1. When you feel comfortable with both parts, you may start learning the solo.

❷❾ SLOW BLUES RHYTHM 2

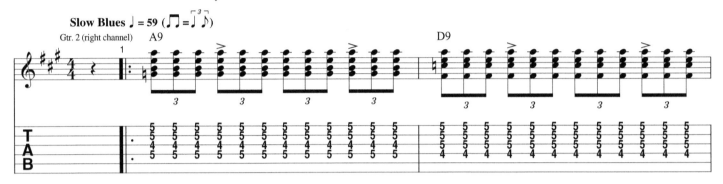

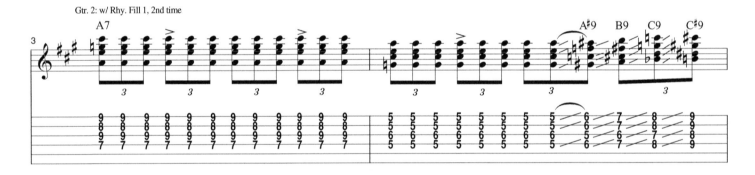

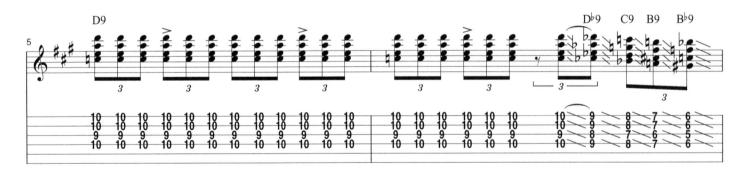

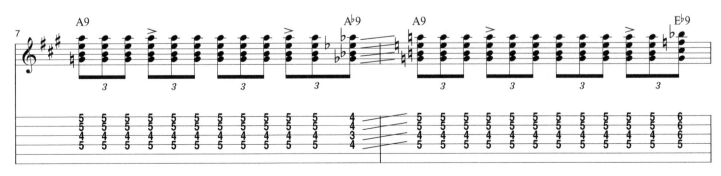

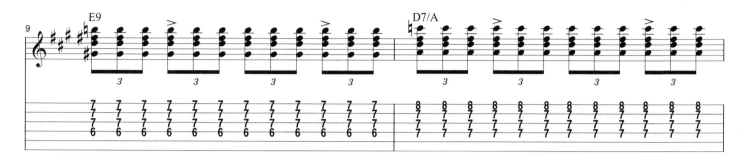

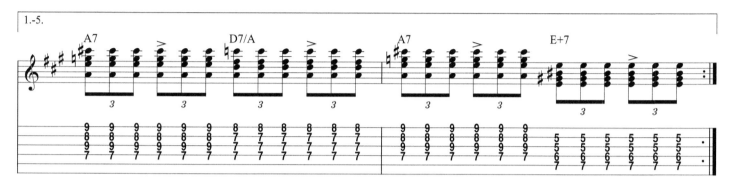

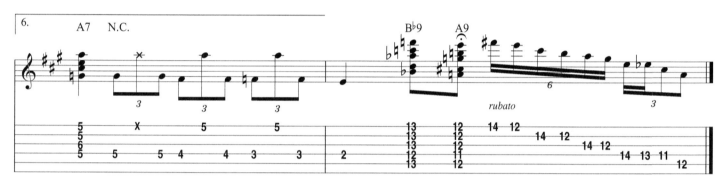

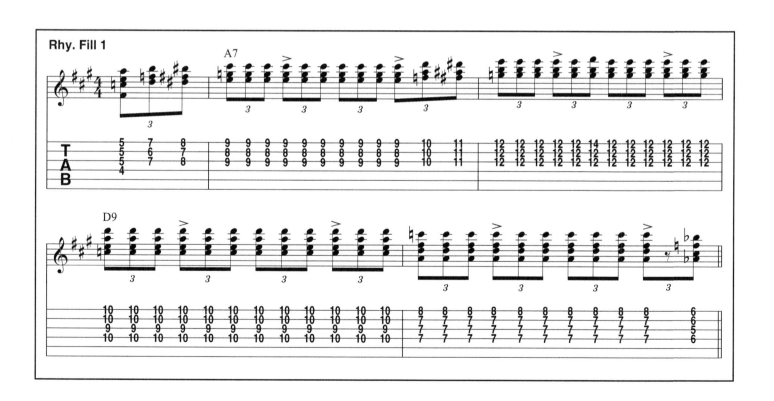

Alternate Voicings

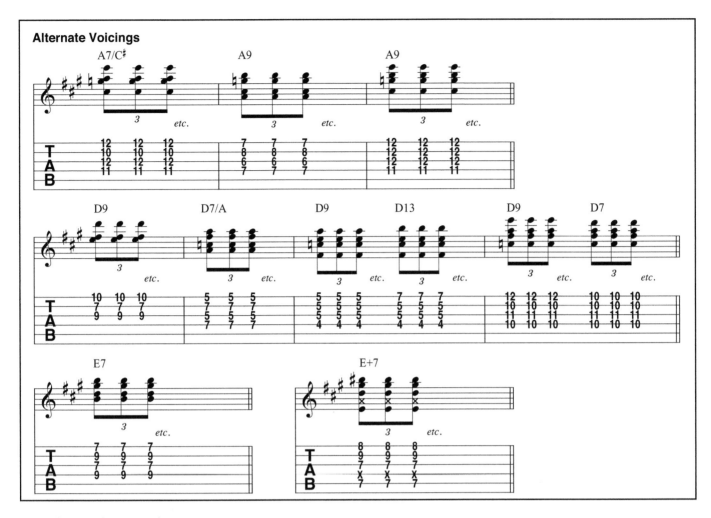

Slow Blues Solo

This solo, also in the key of A, is a little harder than the blues shuffle solo and will take a little more practice to get down. Once again, rely on your ear more than the written transcription to get some of the more subtle nuances. After you have learned the solo, you can use some of the ideas and phrases in your own solos. Try to be creative and come up with your own ideas over the rhythm track.

Chorus 1 opens up with a pickup figure that uses lick 11. Lick 11 is a good way to start a solo and has been used by many great blues players. Measure 2 uses a variation of lick 13 followed by some scale tones and lick 1 on beat 4. Lick 13 is used again in measures 4 and 5. Measures 6 and 7 contain a blues phrase that I originally learned from Johnny Winter and have since heard many other players use. It is one of my favorite blues phrases and one that you should add to your backlog of blues ideas. Beginning on the "and" of beat 3 in measure 8 and continuing into measure 9 is a good lick to play over the V chord (E7 in the key of A). This lick has been used by Albert King, SRV, Johnny Winter, and countless others and is another good lick to add to your vocabulary of blues ideas. Make sure not to overbend the quarter-step bend on the G note which is on beat 4 in measure 9. Measure 10 uses licks 5 and 1 with scale tones. Measure 11 features a good turnaround lick I picked up from Muddy Waters. This one is used by many players and would also be a good lick to add to your vocabulary of blues turnarounds. In measure 12, lick 13 serves as a pickup into the second chorus.

Measures 14 and 15 of chorus 2 contain lick 15. Be sure not to overbend the quarter-step bends on the "and" of beat 4 in measure 14. Listen to the recording to help you get the sound of these quarter-step bends in your head. Measures 16 and 17 contain everyone's favorite, lick 17!! Make sure you nail the minor 3rd bend that starts on beat 3 and that you play the lick in time. Once again, listen closely to the recording to get the sound of it in your head. Lick 16 starts on the "and" of beat 2 in measure 18 and goes into measure 19. A variation of lick 7 is used in measure 20, followed in measure 21 by a variation of the same V chord lick that was in measure 9 of chorus 1. Measure 22 employs another variation of lick 16 while measure 23 repeats the same turnaround lick as in chorus 1, but it is played in seventh position rather than second position. Beat 4 of measure 24 is an Albert King/SRV lick that takes you into the next chorus.

Chorus 3 begins with and includes all of the Albert King/SRV licks and their variations that are in chapter 2. When learning the licks and phrases in measures 25-30, go slowly and make sure your bends and phrasing are accurate. Listen to the recording closely and get the phrasing more from the recording than from the written music. These are great phrases to add to your vocabulary of blues ideas. Measure 28 uses the second half of lick 14. Measures 30 and 31 demonstrate a variation of lick 15 followed by lick 14, which starts on beat 4 of measure 31 and continues into measure 32. Measure 33 contains another V chord lick you should add to your repertoire which is based on a lick very similar to something SRV played. The phrase concludes with lick 1 and slides into lick 16 on the "and" of beat 2 in measure 34. Chorus 3 concludes with the same turnaround lick as chorus 2, with the addition of the partial E7 chord that begins on beat 2 of measure 36 (again something I picked up from Johnny Winter).

Speaking of Mr. Winter, chorus 4 opens up with a very inventive use of lick 2 that I picked up from Johnny and have heard used by a few other players. You can hear Johnny play this lick in his solo on "Third Degree," from the album of the same name (on the Alligator label). A very cool variation of this lick is to ascend in the A Dorian mode (A-B-C-D-E-F♯-G) rather than the A minor pentatonic scale. A variation of lick 4 in measure 40 on beats 3 and 4 end the phrase. Measures 41-43 illustrate an Albert King/SRV-inspired use of lick 8. A very common variation of lick 10 is used in measure 44. Measure 45 contains a variation of lick 4 and lick 1 while measure 46 contains another Albert King/SRV-inspired phrase that leads into the ending lick in measures 47 and 48. This is a very common ending lick that should become part of your bag of blues ending licks. It is a favorite of countless great players and can be heard at the end of thousands (if not millions) of blues tunes. Once again, make sure you do not overbend the quarter-step bends.

◆30 SLOW BLUES SOLO

Chorus 4

*played ahead of the beat

 # Latin Blues

This groove is also referred to as a *blues mamba* or a *blues rhumba*. On a typical blues gig, you will play at least one tune with a Latin feel during the course of the night. This track is based on the tune "Crosscut Saw" by Albert King and is in the key of A. As with the other tracks, the recording has two rhythm guitar parts that you should learn before you start learning the solo. Each rhythm part is hard-panned left and right so they are easy to listen to and practice with.

Rhythm Guitar 1

This part is pretty simple and is very similar to the rhythm part that Jimmie Vaughan played in the tune "Walkin' to My Baby" with the Fabulous Thunderbirds. Make sure you palm mute throughout the entire part and get the accents on the "and" of beat 2 and on beat 4. Stay relaxed, and don't rush! This is a great part that you can use in any tune with a Latin feel. Listen to Gtr. 1's part on the recording, and play along with it. Once you get this part down, you can turn the balance knob on your stereo to the right and play along with Gtr. 2's part.

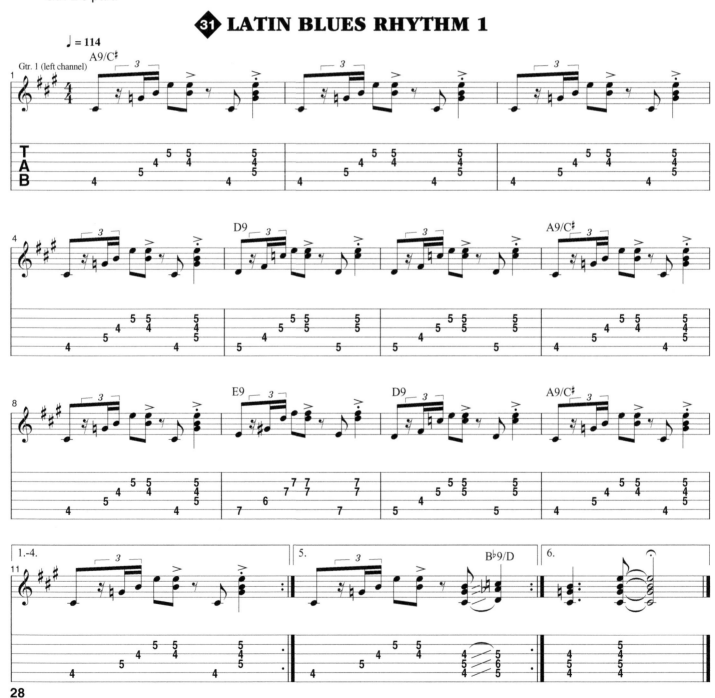

LATIN BLUES RHYTHM 1

Rhythm Guitar 2

This part is very simple, but don't let its simplicity fool you. Play this basic part whenever you are in doubt as to what to play in a given situation. You can never go wrong by playing *backbeats* (playing on beats 2 and 4). Make sure you accent beats 2 and 4 and that you lock in with the drums and don't rush. This part also contains some good chord voicings that you should know. Once you get this part down, you can turn the balance knob on your stereo to the left and play along with Gtr. 1. When you feel comfortable with both parts, you may start learning the solo.

Latin Blues Solo

This solo in the key of A is a little harder than the slow blues solo and will take more practice on your part to get down. Once again, rely on your ear more than the written transcription to get some of the more subtle nuances. This solo is in the style of Albert King and Stevie Ray Vaughan, in addition to containing some licks and phrases from a few other players. After you have learned the solo, you can use some of the ideas and phrases in your own solos. Try to be creative and come up with your own ideas over the rhythm tracks.

Chorus 1 opens up with a pickup figure that is a classic Albert King/SRV lick, which functions as the opening melodic statement for this chorus. Measures 2-4 contain a variation of lick 14 that has been used by countless players and should be very familiar to you. The whole phrase is repeated again, with a very slight variation, in measure 4 and ends on beat 1 in measure 8. A very nice V chord phrase begins on the "and" of 3 in measure 8 and continues into measure 9. Add this one to your blues vocabulary. Once again, don't overbend the quarter-step bends. The trill in measure 12 is also a very nice blues technique you should know. A restatement of the opening melodic phrase serves as a pickup into the second chorus.

Measures 14 and 18 of chorus 2 contain that very famous and ever-popular double-string bend that was developed by Albert King and has been picked up and used by SRV and many others. To play this lick correctly, prebend the note on the first string with your third finger while using your first and second fingers to help support the bend. Catch the second string underneath your third finger and gradually release the bend as you pick the second and first strings. Stevie Ray Vaughan would sometimes catch the first three strings underneath his fingers and then gradually release the bend (listen to "Texas Flood" and "The Sky Is Cryin' "). Try it sometime! Basically, the uglier this lick sounds, the better the effect. Once again, lick 14 is repeated almost as it was in the first chorus in measures 15 and 19. The same V chord lick that was used in the first chorus is repeated again in measures 20 and 21. Also, the same phrase from measures 10 and 11 is repeated in measures 22 and 23.

Chorus 3 begins with a lick sliding into the 6th on the "and" of beat 4 in measure 24. The sixth licks that occur in this chorus were taken from Albert King and utilize both the major and minor 3rd over the I chord. I recommend playing the 6ths with your second and third fingers. The phrase starts with the notes E and C♯ (the 5th and 3rd of A7) and slides down into C and A (the ♭3rd and root of A7). This may sound "wrong" to you at first, but this type of switching from the major 3rd to the minor 3rd over the I chord is very common in the blues. When the IV chord (D9) comes around in measure 29, the 3rd of that chord is avoided, and the ♭7th (C), 5th (A), root (D), and 6th (B) are played instead. Listen carefully to the recording to get the phrasing down for measures 25-32. Another great V chord lick begins on the "and" of beat 3 in measure 32 and continues into measure 33. This is another one that you should memorize. Lick 16 is used in measures 34 and 35, where it is combined with lick 7 on the "and" of beat 4 in measure 35 and continues into measure 36. When playing this lick, make sure you gradually bend from C to C♯.

Chorus 4 opens up with lick 18. Use your first and second fingers when playing this lick, and bend the C note on the second string a quarter step. This lick occurs again in measure 41. Measures 42-46 contain variations of licks 19 and 24 along with some other nice licks and phrases in the style of Johnny Winter. Lick 19 is used in measures 42 and 43 with some notes from the A minor pentatonic scale added to the end of it. Lick 24 is used almost verbatim in measure 46. The hardest phrase to learn and play is the one in measures 45-46. Learn it one group of sixteenth notes at a time. This phrase is a combination of some fairly common blues licks you probably already know or are familiar with but have never played together in this combination. Practice these licks slowly with a metronome or drum machine until you can play the entire phrase up to tempo (114 bpm). Then try playing it along with the recording. The ending lick in measures 47 and 48 is another good one to remember. Use your first finger to play the A notes on both the sixth and first strings in measure 48. This is a technique that was used a lot by SRV.

⬥32 LATIN BLUES SOLO

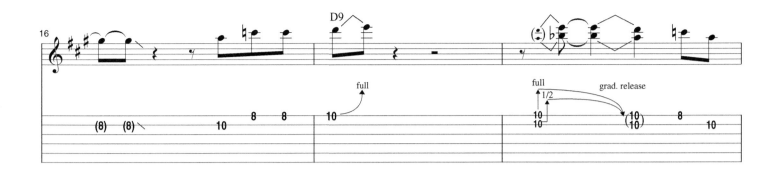

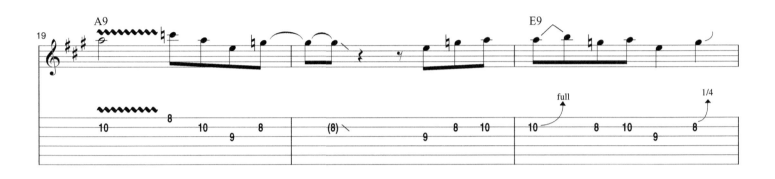

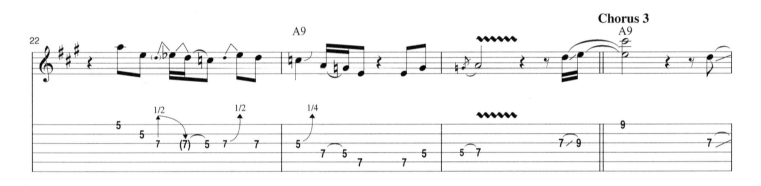

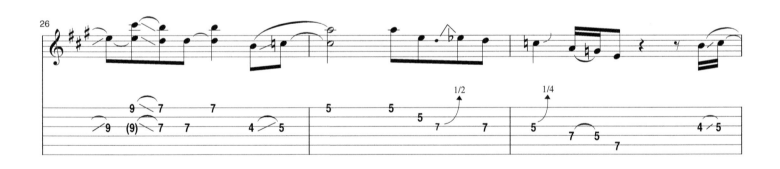

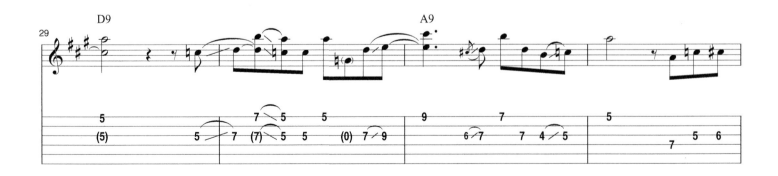

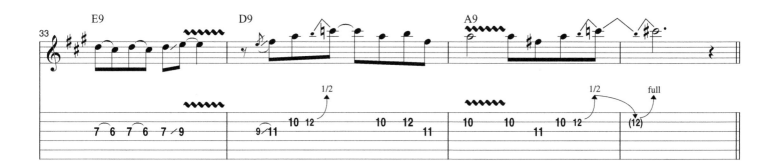

Chorus 4

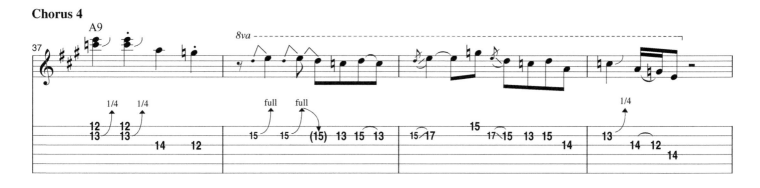

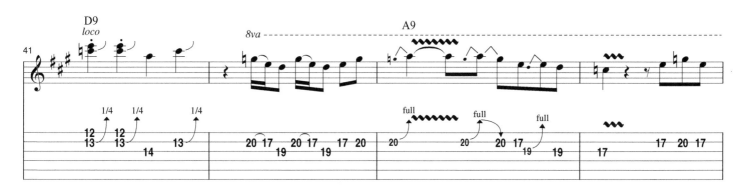

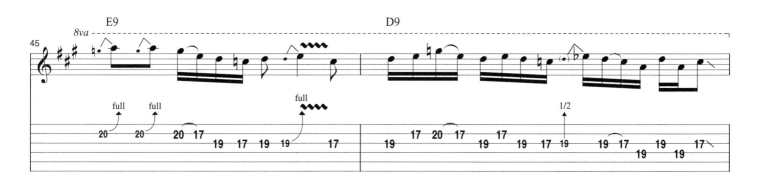

6 Straight Blues

I tried to come up with some kind of creative name for this groove, but I couldn't. "Straight" seemed to be the most descriptive term, plus it is also the one that is commonly used to describe the feel or groove of a tune to a drummer on a gig (*straight* is used to designate the fact that the eighth notes are not swung or shuffled but played "straight"). The groove for this track is based on a tune by Albert Collins called "Get Your Business Straight." You will play this kind of groove almost as much as a shuffle over the course of a blues gig. This track is in the key of C, so you will have to transpose the box positions learned earlier in this book up a minor 3rd (three frets). The rhythm track has three rhythm guitar parts that you should learn before you start learning the solo—Gtr. 1 is on the left channel, Gtr. 2 is panned in the center, and Gtr. 3 is on the right channel.

Rhythm Guitar 1

This part is a pseudo-funk groove because of the sixteenth-note rhythms. Keep your right hand wrist loose, and do not be afraid to hit the strings hard! Make sure you really get that accent on beat 4. Also be aware of the half-step slides into the C9 and F9 chords in measures 2-4, 6, and 8. Do not miss the rest on the "ee" of beat 2—that rest is a very important component of this part. Play the octave turnaround in measures 11 and 12 with all downstrokes. Listen to Gtr 1's part on the recording, and play along with it. Once you get this part down, you can turn the balance knob on your stereo to the right and play along with Gtrs. 2 and 3.

③ STRAIGHT BLUES RHYTHM 1

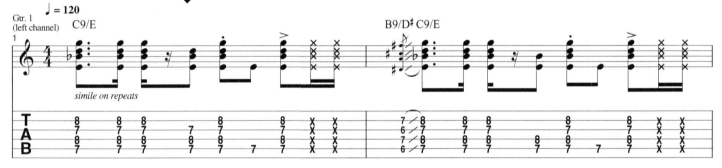

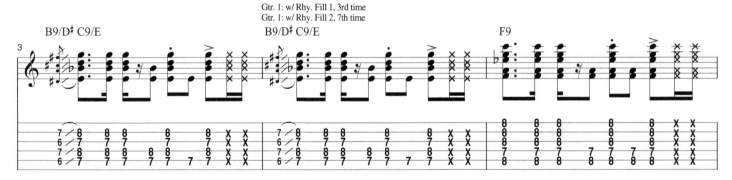

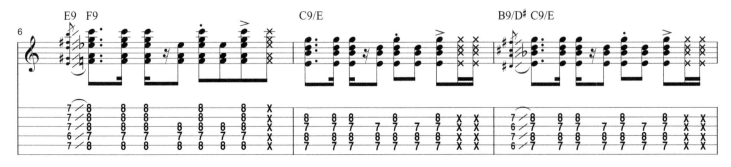

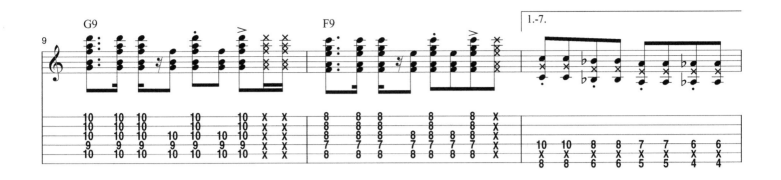

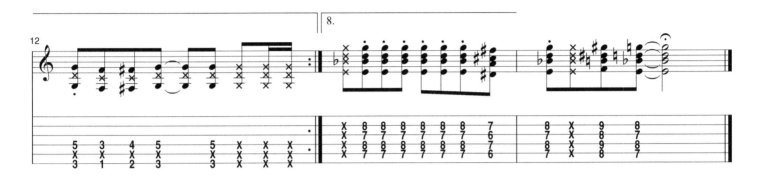

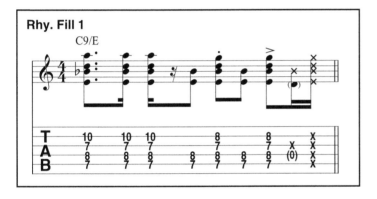

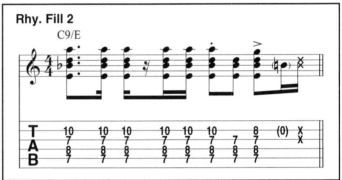

Rhythm Guitar 2

This part is similar to Gtr. 1 and mainly serves to reinforce it. It contains the same voicing of the C9/E chord but is played in second position rather than in seventh position, and is a little more sparse than Gtr. 1. Make sure you get the half-step slides in measures 2-4. Also, make sure you really get those accents on beats 2 and 4. Be aware of the F7 voicing in measures 5, 6, and 10 and the G7/F voicing in measure 9. The chord move from the G7/F (V) chord to the F7 (IV) chord is a really good move to remember. In this part, you can use alternate picking on the turnaround in measures 11 and 12. Once you get this part down, you can turn the balance knob on your stereo to the left and play along with Gtr. 1 or turn it to the right to play along with Gtr. 3. When you feel comfortable with both parts, you may start learning Gtr. 3.

33 ♦ STRAIGHT BLUES RHYTHM 2

Rhythm Guitar 3

This part doubles the bass line with a wah-wah pedal. The wah-wah pedal is optional, so if you don't have one, don't worry about it. Doubling the bass line is another good thing you can do whenever you need to come up with a part but are not sure what to play. Watch the change in the line on the "and" of beat 4 in measures 4, 6, and 8. Also make sure you get the accents on beat 2. As with Gtr. 2, you can use alternate picking on the turnaround in measures 11 and 12. After you get this part down, turn the balance knob on your stereo to the left and play along with Gtr. 1. Once you get all the rhythm parts down, you can start learning the solo.

33 STRAIGHT BLUES RHYTHM 3

Straight Blues Solo

This solo is the hardest one in the book and may take a while for you to learn. It contains a lot of sixteenth-note licks and phrases that go by pretty quickly, so you will have to practice many of the phrases slowly before playing them up to tempo. As with the preceding solos, get the exact phrasing from the recording rather than from the transcription. This solo contains material from Albert Collins, Johnny Winter, Freddie King, and a few others. After you have learned the solos, strive to use some of the ideas and phrases in your own solos. Try to be creative and come up with your own ideas over the rhythm tracks.

Chorus 1 opens up with lick 20 combined with a variation of lick 21 to form the opening melodic statement of this chorus, a statement that ends on beat 1 of measure 4. This phrase is repeated again in measure 4 starting on beat 4 and ends on beat 1 in measure 8. Lick 20 occurs again in measure 8 on beat 4 and is part of a pseudo-Albert King-inspired lick in measure 9 over the V chord. Lick 22 appears in part in measure 10. Lick 22 is used a lot in this solo in various forms. The turnaround lick is doubled in measures 11 and 12 and lick 20 appears again on beat 4 in measure 12 as the start of the melodic statement that takes you into the next chorus.

Chorus 2 begins with part of the same opening statement as the first chorus but departs from it in measure 14 as the idea is developed and expanded upon. The bend from G to A on the "and" of beat 1 in measure 14 is actually a 1¼ step bend. The note you're bending up to is actually a quarter step higher than A. If you just bend up to A, the lick will not sound right. Keep this in mind since this lick is used throughout the solo; every time you see it, make sure you bend up a whole step and a quarter instead of just a whole step. A variation of lick 20 occurs in measure 15 and those pesky sixteenth-note licks start popping up in measure 16. A partial re-statement of the opening melodic statement begins again in measure 16 on beat 4 and is followed by a phrase similar to the one that occurred in measures 14-15. Listen closely to the sixteenth-note variations of lick 22 in measures 21 and 22 in order to get the exact phrasing down.

Things start getting real interesting in chorus 3. This chorus departs from the basic melodic statements of the previous two choruses while increasing the intensity of the solo. Lick 5 opens this chorus up and is followed by some really cool variations of lick 22, which are in the style of Johnny Winter. Lick 1 ends the opening phrase on beat 3 in measure 26. The opening statement is repeated again in measure 27 but is slightly different. Once again, lick 5 starts it off and is again followed by a variation of lick 22 in measure 28 (still in the Winter style). Measure 29 features the same lick as measure 14, but in a different position on the fingerboard. Don't forget that 1 ¼ -step bend! Lick 1 is used again to end the phrase in measure 30 on beat 3. More variations of lick 22 occur in measures 31 and 32. Measure 33 utilizes lick 3 on beat 1 and a variation of lick 21 on beats 2-3. Lick 22 appears again starting on the "ee" of beat 3. Part of lick 14 is used on the "and" of beat 3 in measure 34 and resolves into the turnaround lick in measures 35 and 36.

Chorus 4 features one of my all-time favorite Albert Collins licks. This lick is easy to play and is a great way of adding variety and excitement to your solos. It comes from either the C Dorian or C Mixolydian scales. No matter how you analyze it, play it with conviction and don't rush the quarter-note triplets! I recommend using your left hand pinky to hammer from the A to B♭ in measures 37-40, 43-44, and 47-48; this is a great way to strengthen your pinky. However, you can use your third finger if your fourth finger is too weak.

The tribute to Albert Collins continues into chorus 5 with another great lick from the master of the Telecaster. This stinging lick was actually used by Albert for an entire chorus on his *Live in Japan* album on the tune "Frosty." Here it is only used for the first three and a half measures of this chorus, but I highly recommend trying it for an entire chorus! Attack the string hard, and vibrato that note like there's no tomorrow! The minor 3rd bend from C to E♭ which follows in measures 52 and 53 is also from Mr. Collins and resolves into a variation of lick 1 followed by some more Johnny Winter-inspired licks in measures 54-56, which are variations of lick 22. Measures 57 and 58 feature lick 23, another great lick from Mr. Winter—this is one of my favorites (listen to and read this one closely)—and resolves into the same ending lick that you learned in the slow blues solo except now it is in the key of C.

◆34 STRAIGHT BLUES SOLO

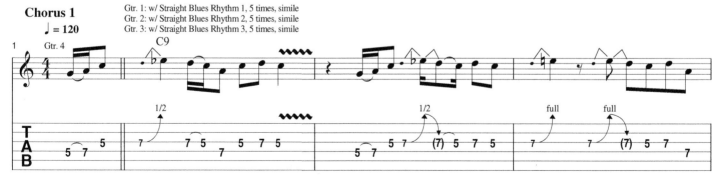

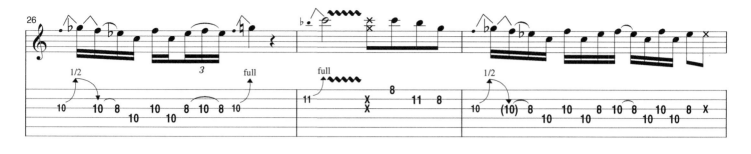

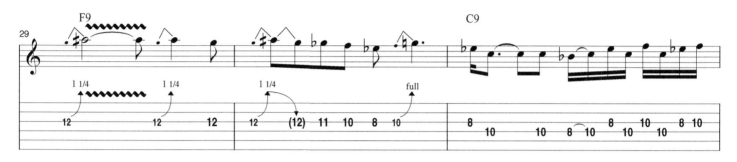

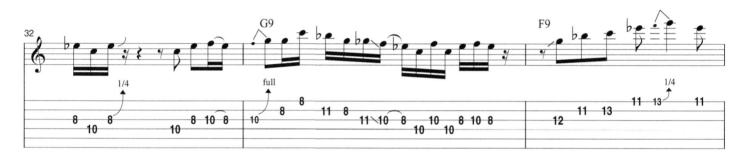

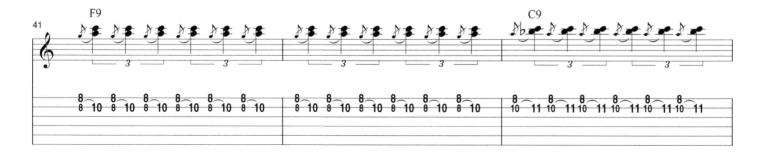

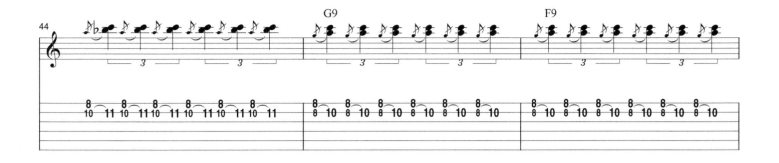

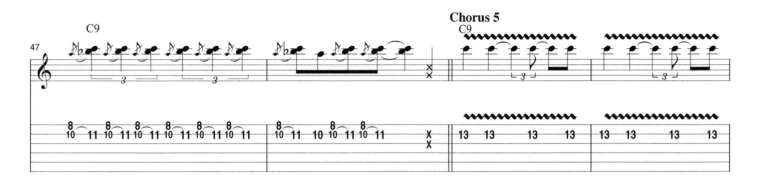

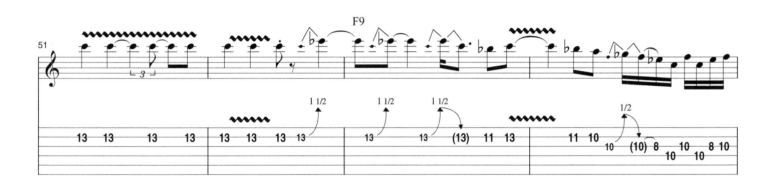

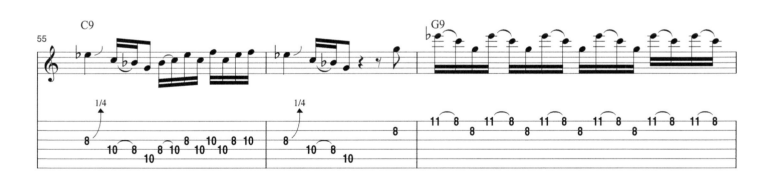

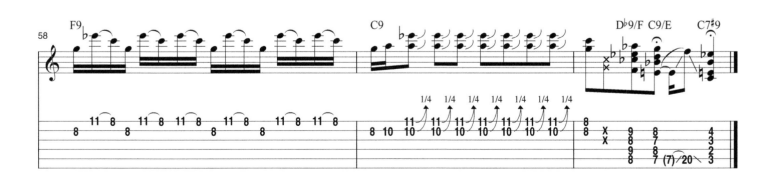

PARTING WORDS

If you have gotten to this point in the book, you have learned both the rhythm parts and the solos to each of the tracks, and you may be wondering what to do next with this information. You now know some good solid rhythm parts to use in a variety of situations, and you have expanded your vocabulary of blues licks and phrases. The next thing to do would be to transpose both the rhythm parts and the solos into different keys. One way to do this would be to start with the more common keys (E, G, D, C) and then transpose to every other key until you can play the parts and solos in all twelve keys. Or, you could start with the key of C and go through the circle of 5ths (C–G–D–A–E–B–F♯–D♭–A♭–E♭–B♭–F). A sequencer could really help you do this, or you could tape yourself playing a rhythm part and then play another rhythm part or the solo over it. Either way, one of your goals as a musician should be to have the ability to play comfortably in all keys, not just the "guitar-friendly" keys. You never know what type of playing situations you will end up in or whom you may end up playing with. After you have transposed everything to every key, the next thing to do would be to take some of the licks and phrases you like from the solos and try playing them over different tracks. For example, you could take the "Straight Blues Solo" (or the parts you like) and play it over the "Latin Blues Rhythm" track and vice versa; you could take the "Blues Shuffle Solo" and play it over the "Latin Blues Rhythm" track; or you could take the "Slow Blues Solo" and play it over the "Blues Shuffle Rhythm" track. This will help develop your creativity as well as help you make those licks and phrases your own. This is a very important part in developing your own musical voice and style. Once you have done this with the material in this book, you should follow the above procedure with every rhythm part, lick, riff, phrase, and solo that you learn!

As you are practicing the solos, you should also work on developing your solo structure. By "solo structure," I mean that your solo should have a discernible beginning, climax, and conclusion. Your solos should say something and go somewhere rather than being a flurry of meaningless notes going nowhere. I like to use the story analogy: a good solo is like a good story in that it has a beginning, some sort of climactic event, and a satisfying conclusion. Ideally, you should start your solo with some sort of melodic idea or statement (also referred to as a *motif* or theme) and develop it over the course of your solo, bringing it to a climax, or point of maximum intensity. You should be able to do this in one chorus, or over two, three, four, five, six, or more choruses. The ability to do this well takes a lot of playing over many years to develop; it doesn't happen overnight! You should be aware of the concept, though, and strive to fulfill it each time you play. The majority of most great blues players follow this basic structure in most of their solos. Another common solo structure form is one that starts out intense, then decreases in intensity, getting quieter with each chorus, and then builds back up in intensity to a level that is higher than where it started. This type of solo is harder to pull off and requires a certain level of musical maturity for it to work. There are numerous variations on these solo structures, but once you develop an intuitive solo structure form in your playing (based on the two models above), you will be on the road to becoming a mature player.

Increasing your vocabulary of blues licks, phrases, and ideas is a never-ending process and is something you should spend the rest of your life doing. I have included a list of albums after this chapter that you can use to further your research into Texas blues. When you hear something you like on a recording, try to learn it and make it a part of your playing.

Above all else, the most important factor in a great solo is feeling the emotion in the notes you play. This is more important than technique or anything else. It's not what you do but how you do what you do that people respond to and either like or don't like. This is the hardest thing to develop because it is not something that can be communicated in a step-by-step procedure—it is very personal and is different for each person. Try to play what you hear and feel at the moment, and constantly strive to play good music. Don't be pretentious and don't try to impress anyone; just play good music and be honest about it. People will respond to you favorably if you try to do this.

Once again, I cannot stress enough the importance of becoming a good, solid rhythm player. We as guitar players seem to spend most of our practice time working on our soloing and sorely neglect our rhythm playing. As a result, many players are good soloists but lousy rhythm players. Since guitarists spend a majority of the time playing rhythm, doesn't it make sense that we work on rhythm playing, too? Of course it does! So, when you are learning things from recordings, learn the rhythm part(s) first before learning the solo(s), just like you learned the material in this book. A great source of rhythm guitar parts that every self-respecting blues player should know can be found in the book *Basic Blues Guitar* by Steve Trovato. I strongly recommend you get this book to further your knowledge of blues rhythm guitar playing.

Finally, the best thing you can do to improve as a player is to play as much as possible either with a friend, play-along tracks like those with this book, a sequencer, or, preferably, a band. This is the single most important thing you can do to accelerate your growth as a musician. So, play, play, play, and play some more!

I hope you have enjoyed working out of this book. Your questions, comments, argumentative statements, and debates regarding the material in this book are welcome. You may write to me in care of Musicians Institute, 1655 McCadden Place, Hollywood, CA 90028. Maybe someday we will get to meet face-to-face. Who knows, maybe we'll end up on a gig together someday—after all, this is a strange business! Don't forget to keep on pickin' and a grinnin'!!

RECOMMENDED LISTENING

The following list of albums comes from my personal collection and should give you a good start on Texas blues music and some of the better artists. This list is by no means exhaustive and is intended just as a primer. Hopefully your own personal collection will become much larger than this. So, without any further ado...

1. *Blues Masters, Vol. 3: Texas Blues*, Rhino R2 71123

2. T-Bone Walker: *The Complete Imperial Recordings, 1950-1954*, EMI

3. Freddy King: *Just Pickin'*, Modern Blues

4. Although you cannot go wrong with any Johnny Winter album, most of his albums on Columbia and Blue Sky were not straight-ahead blues albums. All of those albums contain some great blues tunes (and are worth getting), but if you want to hear some of Johnny's best blues playing, I highly recommend the following albums:

a. *Guitar Slinger,* Alligator

b. *Serious Business,* Alligator

c. *Third Degree,* Alligator

d. *Let Me In,* Pointblank

e. *Hey, Where's Your Brother,* Pointblank

5. As with Johnny Winter, you can't go wrong with any Stevie Ray Vaughan album. The following are the ones I recommend:

a. *Texas Flood,* Epic

b. *Soul to Soul,* Epic

c *In Step,* Epic

d. *The Sky Is Cryin',* Epic

6. *The Essential Fabulous Thunderbirds Collection,* Chrysalis

7. Albert Collins, Robert Cray, Johnny Copeland: *Showdown,* Alligator ALCD 4743 (two out of three ain't bad)

8. Albert Collins: *Cold Snap,* Alligator ALCD 4752

The following is a list of what I consider essential recordings from some non-Texas blues musicians who have influenced many Texas blues players including some of the ones listed above. As with the previous list, this list is not by any means exhaustive:

1. Albert King: *The Ultimate Collection,* Rhino

2. B.B. King: *King of the Blues,* box set MCA

3. B.B. King: *Live at the Regal,* MCA

4. Muddy Waters: *The Chess Box*

5. The following Muddy Waters albums were produced by Johnny Winter and, in addition to being some of Muddy's best work, also include some fine playing from Mr. Winter:

a. *Hard Again,* Blue Sky

b. *I'm Ready,* Blue Sky

c. *Muddy "Mississippi" Waters Live,* Blue Sky

d. *King Bee,* Blue Sky

ABOUT THE AUTHOR

Robert Calva began playing guitar in Houston, Texas. It was not long before he discovered the blues and realized that it was the music he most wanted to play. Robert has studied music at the University of North Texas and at Musicians Institute. While a student at MI, Robert was given the Outstanding Student of the Year Award for 1991-'92. Robert began teaching at MI in 1993. He has played with Bo Diddley, Tim Bogert, Deacon Jones, Joe Houston, and countless others. He currently teaches at MI and at Delian Music in Culver City, CA. In addition to this he performs in and around Southern California with his band, Terri and the T-Bones.

ABOUT THE AUDIO

The audio was recorded and mixed by Paul Hanson at Across The Sound Studio in Santa Clarita, CA. Jack McKenty played bass on it and yours truly played all the guitar parts. The audio was produced by Paul Hanson and myself. For you tone hounds, I played all the tracks on my 1988 Fender American Standard Strat through a '59 Fender re-issue Bassman. For effects I used a '63 Fender re-issue tank reverb unit and an Ibanez re-issue TS-9 Tube Screamer.

Guitar Notation Legend

Guitar Music can be notated three different ways: on a *musical staff*, in *tablature*, and in *rhythm slashes*.

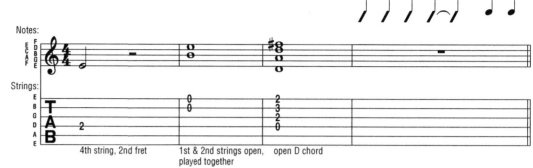

RHYTHM SLASHES are written above the staff. Strum chords in the rhythm indicated. Use the chord diagrams found at the top of the first page of the transcription for the appropriate chord voicings. Round noteheads indicate single notes.

THE MUSICAL STAFF shows pitches and rhythms and is divided by bar lines into measures. Pitches are named after the first seven letters of the alphabet.

TABLATURE graphically represents the guitar fingerboard. Each horizontal line represents a string, and each number represents a fret.

Notes:

Strings:

4th string, 2nd fret   1st & 2nd strings open,   open D chord
played together

HALF-STEP BEND: Strike the note and bend up 1/2 step.

WHOLE-STEP BEND: Strike the note and bend up one step.

GRACE NOTE BEND: Strike the note and bend up as indicated. The first note does not take up any time.

SLIGHT (MICROTONE) BEND: Strike the note and bend up 1/4 step.

BEND AND RELEASE: Strike the note and bend up as indicated, then release back to the original note. Only the first note is struck.

PRE-BEND: Bend the note as indicated, then strike it.

VIBRATO: The string is vibrated by rapidly bending and releasing the note with the fretting hand.

WIDE VIBRATO: The pitch is varied to a greater degree by vibrating with the fretting hand.

HAMMER-ON: Strike the first (lower) note with one finger, then sound the higher note (on the same string) with another finger by fretting it without picking.

PULL-OFF: Place both fingers on the notes to be sounded. Strike the first note and without picking, pull the finger off to sound the second (lower) note.

LEGATO SLIDE: Strike the first note and then slide the same fret-hand finger up or down to the second note. The second note is not struck.

SHIFT SLIDE: Same as legato slide, except the second note is struck.

TRILL: Very rapidly alternate between the notes indicated by continuously hammering on and pulling off.

TAPPING: Hammer ("tap") the fret indicated with the pick-hand index or middle finger and pull off to the note fretted by the fret hand.

NATURAL HARMONIC: Strike the note while the fret-hand lightly touches the string directly over the fret indicated.

PINCH HARMONIC: The note is fretted normally and a harmonic is produced by adding the edge of the thumb or the tip of the index finger of the pick hand to the normal pick attack.

PICK SCRAPE: The edge of the pick is rubbed down (or up) the string, producing a scratchy sound.

MUFFLED STRINGS: A percussive sound is produced by laying the fret hand across the string(s) without depressing, and striking them with the pick hand.

PALM MUTING: The note is partially muted by the pick hand lightly touching the string(s) just before the bridge.

RAKE: Drag the pick across the strings indicated with a single motion.

TREMOLO PICKING: The note is picked as rapidly and continuously as possible.

VIBRATO BAR DIVE AND RETURN: The pitch of the note or chord is dropped a specified number of steps (in rhythm) then returned to the original pitch.

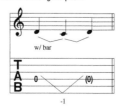

VIBRATO BAR SCOOP: Depress the bar just before striking the note, then quickly release the bar.

VIBRATO BAR DIP: Strike the note and then immediately drop a specified number of steps, then release back to the original pitch.

46

MUSICIANS INSTITUTE PRESS is the official series of Southern California's renowned music school, Musicians Institute. MI instructors, some of the finest musicians in the world, share their vast knowledge and experience with you – no matter what your current level. For guitar, bass, drums, vocals, and keyboards, MI Press offers the finest music curriculum for higher learning through a variety of series:

ESSENTIAL CONCEPTS	**MASTER CLASS**	**PRIVATE LESSONS**
Designed from MI core curriculum programs.	*Designed from MI elective courses.*	*Tackle a variety of topics "one-on one" with MI faculty instructors.*

GUITAR

Acoustic Artistry
by Evan Hirschelman • **Private Lessons**
00695922 Book/Online Audio $24.99

Advanced Scale Concepts & Licks for Guitar
by Jean Marc Belkadi • **Private Lessons**
00695298 Book/CD Pack $22.99

All-in-One Guitar Soloing Course
by Daniel Gilbert & Beth Marlis
00217709 Book/Online Media $29.99

Blues/Rock Soloing for Guitar
by Robert Calva • **Private Lessons**
00695680 Book/Online Audio $22.99

Blues Guitar Soloing
by Keith Wyatt • **Master Class**
00695132 Book/Online Audio $29.99

Blues Rhythm Guitar
by Keith Wyatt • **Master Class**
00695131 Book/Online Audio $22.99

Dean Brown
00696002 DVD $29.95

Chord Progressions for Guitar
by Tom Kolb • **Private Lessons**
00695664 Book/Online Audio $19.99

Chord Tone Soloing
by Barrett Tagliarino • **Private Lessons**
00695855 Book/Online Audio $27.99

Chord-Melody Guitar
by Bruce Buckingham • **Private Lessons**
00695646 Book/Online Audio $22.99

Classical & Fingerstyle Guitar Techniques
by David Oakes • **Master Class**
00695171 Book/Online Audio $22.99

Classical Themes for Electric Guitar
by Jean Marc Belkadi • **Private Lessons**
00695806 Book/CD Pack $15.99

Country Guitar
by Al Bonhomme • **Master Class**
00695661 Book/Online Audio $22.99

Essential Rhythm Guitar
by Steve Trovato • **Private Lessons**
00695181 Book/CD Pack $16.99

Exotic Scales & Licks for Electric Guitar
by Jean Marc Belkadi • **Private Lessons**
00695860 Book/CD Pack $19.99

Funk Guitar
by Ross Bolton • **Private Lessons**
00695419 Book/Online Audio $17.99

Guitar Basics
by Bruce Buckingham • **Private Lessons**
00695134 Book/Online Audio $19.99

Guitar Fretboard Workbook
by Barrett Tagliarino • **Essential Concepts**
00695712 . . . . $22.99

Guitar Hanon
by Peter Deneff • **Private Lessons**
00695321 . . . . $17.99

Guitar Lick•tionary
by Dave Hill • **Private Lessons**
00695482 Book/CD Pack $22.99

Guitar Soloing
by Dan Gilbert & Beth Marlis • **Essential Concepts**
00695190 Book/Online Audio $24.99

Harmonics
by Jamie Findlay • **Private Lessons**
00695169 Book/CD Pack $16.99

Harmony & Theory
by Keith Wyatt & Carl Schroeder • **Essential Concepts**
00695161 . . . . $24.99

Introduction to Jazz Guitar Soloing
by Joe Elliott • **Master Class**
00695406 Book/Online Audio $24.99

Jazz Guitar Chord System
by Scott Henderson • **Private Lessons**
00695291 . . . . $14.99

Jazz Guitar Improvisation
by Sid Jacobs • **Master Class**
00217711 Book/Online Media $19.99

Jazz, Rock & Funk Guitar
by Dean Brown • **Private Lessons**
00217690 Book/Online Media $19.99

Latin Guitar
by Bruce Buckingham • **Master Class**
00695379 Book/Online Audio $19.99

Lead Sheet Bible
by Robin Randall & Janice Peterson • **Private Lessons**
00695130 Book/Online Audio $24.99

Liquid Legato
by Allen Hinds • **Private Lessons**
00696656 Book/Online Audio $17.99

Modern Jazz Concepts for Guitar
by Sid Jacobs • **Master Class**
00695711 Book/CD Pack $19.99

Modern Rock Rhythm Guitar
by Danny Gill • **Private Lessons**
00695682 Book/Online Audio $22.99

Modes for Guitar
by Tom Kolb • **Private Lessons**
00695555 Book/Online Audio $19.99

Music Reading for Guitar
by David Oakes • **Essential Concepts**
00695192 . . . . $24.99

Outside Guitar Licks
by Jean Marc Belkadi • **Private Lessons**
00695697 Book/CD Pack $16.99

Power Plucking
by Dale Turner • **Private Lesson**
00695962 Book/CD Pack $19.95

Progressive Tapping Licks
by Jean Marc Belkadi • **Private Lessons**
00695748 Book/CD Pack $19.99

Rhythm Guitar
by Bruce Buckingham & Eric Paschal • **Essential Concepts**
00695188 Book $22.99
00114559 Book/Online Audio $27.99
00695909 DVD $19.95

Rhythmic Lead Guitar
by Barrett Tagliarino • **Private Lessons**
00110263 Book/Online Audio $22.99

Rock Lead Basics
by Nick Nolan & Danny Gill • **Master Class**
00695144 Book/Online Audio $19.99

Rock Lead Performance
by Nick Nolan & Danny Gill • **Master Class**
00695278 Book/Online Audio $19.99

Rock Lead Techniques
by Nick Nolan & Danny Gill • **Master Class**
00695146 Book/Online Audio $19.99

Shred Guitar
by Greg Harrison • **Master Class**
00695977 Book/Online Audio $24.99

Solo Slap Guitar
by Jude Gold • **Master Class**
00139556 Book/Online Video $24.99

Technique Exercises for Guitar
by Jean Marc Belkadi • **Private Lessons**
00695913 Book/CD Pack $17.99

Texas Blues Guitar
by Robert Calva • **Private Lessons**
00695340 Book/Online Audio $19.99

Ultimate Guitar Technique
by Bill LaFleur • **Private Lessons**
00695863 Book/Online Audio $24.99

Prices, contents, and availability subject to change without notice.

HAL•LEONARD®

7777 W. BLUEMOUND RD. P.O. BOX 13819 MILWAUKEE, WI 53213

www.halleonard.com